THE GLIMPSE OF INDIAN EDUCATION

VIVEKA VARDHAN NAIDU BHYRIPUDI

XpressPublishing

An imprint of Notion Press

XpressPublishing
An imprint of Notion Press

No.8, 3rd Cross Street,CIT Colony,
Mylapore, Chennai, Tamil Nadu-600004

ISBN 978-1-64919-220-2

I dedicate this book to my parents for supporting me to move in the path of my interests and my lecturers, **Sri B.Sambasiva Rao** and **Sri U.Ranjith kumar,** who made me realise the real meaning of education.

Contents

Foreword

I am delighted to write the foreword of the first work of my companion regarding the educational practices in India. Basically, being students, we both regularly had conversations regarding the subject and the study patterns we follow. After getting habituated to the study environment, we felt suffocated with the procedures and patterns we were following, in order to get educated. We always thought of the real meaning of education which is very difficult to understand. Once, the author read a question generated by a netizen in quora......

"If digitalization makes India productive and developed, what will be the first thing you would suggest to be digitalized?" and he answered "Education" should be given the major priority to be digitalized so that every individual of India shows interest to get educated. But, the main questions arised at that moment.

1. "Does the thing what we call education, meet the required standards that lead to the development of our Country?"
2. "How does the educations patterns,that we are following, contribute to the development of national Integrity?"

These two questions made a challenge and motivated him to find the ideas to reconstruct the education system and he had a great support from his lecturer **Sri B.Sambasiva Rao.** All his ideas is to gift a healthy and prospective education to the future generation and construct a backbone for the real development of the nation, that fulfills the dream of Sir A. P. J. Abdul Kalam.

Sai mohan Nandigama

Preface

This book was written by me during the lockdown period, just to signify the term "Education" and to reveal the real meaning of it. Though I am a student pursuing by Degree, I wanted to express my thoughts and Ideas, regarding how our education sysytem should be. To be Frank, it appears disgusting to the parents who are thinking that Engineering and Medicine are the only professions , but they should know the real fact.

Even, I wanted each and every child, pursuing his education, to know the real meaning of the education and study environment he was exposed to. I must express my gratitude to my classmates and friends, for the innumerable talks and late night discussions we had during this lock down period, which made my thoughts to cover the major concepts of the Ethical work, "pursuing an education that is meaningful".

This work involves the real life situations we (me and my associates who were involved in this work) faced in this real world and the society, where the people think answering a question by a continuous reading and getting 100% marks is an achievement. Not every person is supposed to be loved by everyone and not every literary work and thesis work should be accepted by everyone. I don't think that everyone gets connected to my work, but I can proudly say that the people who accept my writeup are the one who is willing to have a healthy society.

Though, the work is mine, it depicts the thoughts and real struggle of millions of students. The ideas they have, the misconceptions they were judged by, the mental pressure they were facing and such concepts are brought into context to bring them forward.

Viveka Vardhan Naidu Bhyripudi

1

Divine Education of Ancient India

India, the nation of "Unity in Diversity", is well known for the education practices that were implemented in ancient education patterns. That's the reason, why India had a nickname, "**Knowledge Hub of the World**". Nalanda university stands as the best example to support the statement. It was remained the best for 800 years with 10,000 students from many countries like Korea, Japan, China, Indonesia, persia and other. Nalanda university was best known for its teaching of Vedas along with science and ethics. This factor made it unique and made it international reknown.

Those ashramas, the pleasant environment, the dedication of the teachers in those days made India, the land of intellectuals. Rather than studying from the books, people at those days, learned the lessons from the nature, thats why, the feeling "**Nature is the best teacher**" had a great impact even today. This idea laid road to the establishment of Shantiniketan, the educational institution, that directly linked with the nature, which is said to be the mastepiece of Rabindranath Tagore. His contribution brought the ancient and old feelings of "**guru-sishya relation and universal brotherhood**" back into existence.

These solid structures denote the most prominent and standard education at the past. But, as time lapsed....these structures got ruined in the wars just like the decline of education levels of our country. I just don't say it got ruined but, it has changed its motto and the basic principle. Vedas convey the importance of honesty and hardwork in achieving a goal and the present studies were concentrating on a term **"Smart work"** and **"Closed room study"**.......

Everything seems to create a dilemma in your minds........Isn't it, readers?.... Let's move on, to experience the present...... Let's get the things known from the real life incidents, which we often find in news channels and news papers.

 his

2
The true diaries

The more we get interacted with the nature, the more we learn. This helps in increasing the potential to think out of the box......but, getting stucked under the closed room coorporate education jungle, the students dont even find a way to express their ideas, which got stucked in their brains, waiting for the right time. The reality is this never happen because, their thoughts are being suppressed by the so called "Advanced learning techniques", implemented by the so called educationists. I remember my school days, the best memories of my life, where I used to spend the time thinking about the stories I used to read in our school library, the moments we enjoyed during the Games period, the chit-chats we had during the leisure time.

Besides subject, we used to develop *Aesthetics*. This is possible, due to the correlation between the student and the nature. But, the schools of today don't even have a Play ground, as the management thinks allowing the students to play, is a time waste process. All that they need is a continuous study and an advertisement for top ranks, no matter whatever the pressure and stress the student were feeling. I will never say that it's the mistake of the management. "Need creates the emergence" is the universal truth that comes into context, signifying the emergence of colleges in abound. The need of the parents to make their children make their way to IIT's, NIT's, AIIMS and other top class institutions, paved a path to the emergence of Corporate educational institutions.

The roads on Sunday, which was filled with children holding bats, are replaced by empty roads showing the way to tutions and coaching academies. The leisure time turned busy with the assignments and works. Book bags are replaced by book sacks, which in my view is the major burden for the growing children, causing physical and mental problems at the young age. Not even the schools, but also colleges, universities and other educational institutions are working on a production activity of producing Robots, but not a civilised citizen.

An Educational institution should be a support to the student but, it should never be a burden, because, students spend most of the time in the schools and colleges itself. This is the second home to the students and it,s all a family. After getting settled, a smile should be observed on the faces while remembering their school days. I has become difficult to differentiate a school from a jail, based on the activities that are being performed in the community.

1.   **What do you people observe in the present education community ?...........**

2.   **Is this standard sufficient to create a good nation and healthy future?.........**

3.   **How does the future linked with the present education practices?..........**

These 3 questions are considered to be the most important aspects that are to be concentrated, in my view and my opinion as well, because, all the actives that we are carrying out at present is to build our lives. Let's get the answers from the daily life incidents and from the people we meet. It may be our parents, our friends, our relatives, our siblings, our acquaintance. Everyone's life is an experience, which teaches the best lessons of life. That's the only reason, why our parents say,

""Just experience the fact and truth. It teaches you the best lesson, that you will never forget"........."

Dream of a school kid

I used to look at the coaching centres, lying on the roadside, which provides training for Engineering and Medical entrance examination. What makes me laugh and feel pity is, school children driven forcefully by their parents into the class rooms. A question usually strikes my brain,"**How can a school kid understand and remember the subject which is even harder to remember by the college students?**". The answer I got from my inner voice is "**They should remember..no matter how hard it is**"..

One day, on my way to college, which is 7km from my residential area, I found my neighbour kid and his mother standing under the tree. I went near them and asked whether they need any help. His mom replied " Charan missed his school bus, Vivek. So, I am waiting for an auto, to drop him at the school". I remember that his school is situated at the road next to my college. So, I said her mother that I would drop him at the school. His mother felt thankful.

We both started our journey. charan is a 6th class student. I asked him " Charan, what is the name of your school?" and he replied "Akshara IIT academy"......."You are also the one among million sufferrers", I said to myself in a low voice. "What subjects they teach you?", asked him. He said,   "Along with the academic subjects, they teach us techno subjects like Basics of Kinematics, Rotational Dynamics and General physics". Listening to his answer, I got suffocated and felt pity of him....

"Do you really want to become an Engineer?", I asked to know whether he joined here willingly. "No, I never wanted to become an Engineer. I dreamed to become an Army officer but my parents refused." charan replied with a dull voice. "What made your parents refuse?", asked him to know the reason. "Its all due to my cousin Aravind. He scored good marks in the engineering entrance test and got seat at IIT Delhi. My parents wanted me to study engineering at good IIT's though it's not my interest. They forced me to join in this school so that I could get a good score and join in any of the IIT's.", Charan replied and I can find the pain behind his words....

I dropped him at his school and went to my college. Though I was in my class room with murmuring and chit chatting sounds of my classmates, I was thinking about the pain and stress charan was bearing at a very small age. Rather than fighting with the enemies at the border, he was fighting with the ideology of his parents, without even uttering a word. I observed the respect given to his parents, in his words and also found the cruelty of his parents. I don't term it as cruelty, but it is their vision to look his son at top most position.

This is not just the story of Charan, but it is the real situation, which is being faced by each and every student of India. All this is just because of lack of understanding capability among the parent community. "If others can do it, why can't you?", the most familiar question the parents ask their children, especially in a country like India........

The answer that comes to the mind is "Yes, I can do it...but, I don't wanna do it because, I am not interested". There comes the most famous character in the middle, "The Fear". The fear of what parents think about them, the fear of friends bullying, the fear of how the relatives react to his failure...........All these thoughts surround his dreams and makes him timid. In my view, they are timid and they will be timid, even they score good marks in the entrances and secure good seats at the best institutions, because of their inability to express their ideas and dreams, which makes him abortive in his dream world.

Is education a business?

Education, the art of expressing the ideas and concepts of life with ethics and human values, became a commercial source for the money makers. The epics of "Ramayana and Mahabharata" stated that, Interest and perseverance are the only capital to invest, but Money had the lion's share to promote and pursue education in the present developing world, especially in India. Looking at the coaching institutions and training academies, at first, I used to think "How dedicated these people are. They are trying very hard to make our Country a developed nation in terms of Education" gazing at the walls covered with the thought provoking words of many great people. Later, I realised that those words are just confined to walls, not the people and the society.

One day, during the newspaper session, my eyes went through an advertisement**"Bonanza for IIT and NEET aspirants", an introduction session by the famous Psychologist**. Though I was not an IIT or NEET aspirant, I was fascinated to hear his lecture regarding the tips to remember the concepts of difficult subjects, so that, it will be helpful for the future purposes. I made myself free on the day of lecture and went to the seminar hall, which was 3 km from the place I reside.

The session started with the introduction of the guest. The guest started giving his lecture, how important IIT'S and Medical entrances became prominent in everyone's life. Later, he asked the crowd to tell the last two digits of their phone number in random and filled those digits in a 10*10 grid. After completing filling the grid, he challenged the crowd to ask any number among the grid, so that he would tell the exact grid location of the number. He answered the correct locations of the numbers placed in the grid. Everyone in the seminar hall got surprised with his skills.

Later he said, "This is how I am going to train your kinds. No matter how hard, how complex the task is, I will provide them the ability to solve it within less time. All you need is just a registration with a payment of Rs.7,000 for a 7 day session. You will experience the best transformation in your child. So be quick".....and I found people running towards the registration desk....

I laughed in myself looking at the flock of sheep, blindly following a slaughterer."**Rs.7000 for a seven day session...!!!why such a huge amount just to train our brains?**", my inner voice questioned me. **Can't we train our brains on our own? Why to depend on someone else to make our brain listen to our words? Did great people like Swami Vivekananda, Ramakrishna paramahamsa, Einstein, C.V. Raman and many, took help of such people to train their ideas?**....These questions started occupying my brain, that made me mad. The fact is, though we are capable in doing so, we are lazy to do it and finds for the simple ways shown by others. This is what the poeple of India call " A success".

"How much did you work to get a successful result?" became an old form of addressing a successful person. "If you did not spend more money, how can you be successful?" is the new era question...........

The letter of a failure

       One day, I had a phonecall from my friend Pranav. I woke up, lifted the call and felt heartbreak with his words. The news was regarding the death of my friend, Harini. She was the topper of our class. She was the state topper in SSC examination. She wanted to become a lawyer, and she always wanted to help the people and the society. Life is not as simple as we think....... She was forced by her father to join in the stream of BiPC. She tried to convince her father but his father never cared her words.

       She tried her level best to score in the model tests conducted by the college, but always scored less marks. Gradually, her father started to pressure her to make her mind to study, even during vacation. Sometimes, she cried during the call with me. I always tried to comfort her, but I knew that it's easy to give a suggestion but it is very hard to bear the situation. Frankly speaking, I have never seen her smiling heartfully during the time we met. I felt she was brave but her suicide made me feel I was wrong.

       I reached her home along with Pranav. I was still unable to accept the truth of her death but her dead body laid on the coffin, made me realize the sad truth of her absence on the earth. I looked at her father sobbing "It's all my mistake, Harini". I comforted her father and said,"It's not at all your mistake uncle. Please stop crying. Be brave". He replied, "It's my mistake, Vivek. I never gave importance to her ideas and thoughts. I was just a money machine in her life, providing all the facilities she needed but not the father's love. That's the only reason for her death". This made me cry but his realization can't bring Harini alive. Then, his father handed me a letter written by Harini.

       I felt tensed to open the letter and read the last words of Harini. I wanted Harini with a smiling face and her braveness to be lasted in my memory. Atlast, I changed my mind and started reading the letter, just to feel her last words.

"

Dear dad

I know, you wanted me to become a doctor. I also know that you love me so much. You worked hard and sacrificed your life just to make my life beautiful, but I am sorry I am incapable to fulfill your dream. I tried the best I could, but I am unable to do this which is quiet different from my dream. I remember the day when you stopped talking to me, when I scored fewer marks in the academics. I can't live a moment without talking to you........I always wanted happiness to be filled in your eyes. Later, I realised that my presence as a failure, won't make you happy. My father should not be the father of a failure kid. But I had no chance to become a successful person. So, I decided to end my life as a failure.

A letter from your Failure daughter................
"

Tears rolled down my eyes revealing the truth that Harini was no more with us. She could be a successful lawyer like Madam Fathima Beevi but ended her life with an appearance of dead corpse in front of my eyes, just like a failure ....

The comparison

"**Comparison**" ... is used as the major criteria to judge the success rate of a person. Parents start expressing their ideas, "**He scored very good marks... She made a good move in her medical entrance.... He scored a good percentage in his academics.... He achieved the seat in AIIMS.....He got selected in the campus recruitment with so and so package.....He made this.....She made that..............**" and all these statements end with an universal question, "**Why didn't you get that....?**", which directly affects the confidence level. This became so adverse that even the teachers and mentors started comparing students with the fellow people.

I remember the day, when my friend Rehanth wept before me, thinking of the words of his class teacher. Rehanth was the member of a Robotic community of his college, which worked on the development of advanced robotic technologies. The community was quite different from the college environment where there will be no professors or mentors. Everything and every activity was carried under student control, with the permissions of the management. Working on a project to make it enable for public use, they spent 2 weeks to develop it, without attending the classes.

At last, they had completed the report and model submissions. Their routine college life started and everything was good. At that moment, due to low attendance, he was called by his mentor to give the reason. He had submitted every proof and permission letters issued by the management. His mentor, taking the letters, said, "**While everyone are engaged with their studies, even Arjun (the topper guy), what made you to involve in these activities? Can't you stay aside from them? Take some suggestions from Arjun and at least score average marks....**"......

Rehanth was speechless. He just smiled and said,"**Yes sir, thanks for your suggestion**" but, I can feel the pain behind his words. According to the 3rd law of Newton, each and every action has a reaction. Rehanth's project got selected for National demonstration and everyone started praising his achievement. His mentor called him to his cabin and wished him for his success. Rehanth, with a smiley face said, **"Just suggest Arjun to explore the world, sir. Otherwise, he would end his life in a closed cabin, compiling programs and judging others, just like you...."**

This real life experience made me realize not to judge anyone with the marks or with other aspects, because, time never let those judgements last long. Most of the suicide deaths in India were due to low confidence levels and, they find no one as a support, which leads to the most dangerous mental imbalance, **"Depression".** Parents should be the saviour of their child but they don't know the reality, where their child was thinking them as traitor. Each and everyone is gifted with their inborn talents which make them unique. All that they require is the support to get accessed with his ideas of development.

Education and Politics

"..........today, everything is commercialized- politics, religion, education, ideology, belief, the armed services........Everything has its price

-Carroll Quigley "

"A well educated persons has the ability to turn into a good leader, shaping a good nation". This is what our epics taught. The present day situation is quiet irrelatable with this concept. If anyone has a desire to become a leader or a politician, all that he require is huge sums of money, where his education skills and academic performances are thought to be useless. It became very hard to get into any profession like an engineer or a doctor rather than becoming a politician.

A startup named "Vision India", planned an education activity of explaining the emerging technologies in the world to the college students. Activities and tasks are distributed among the group volunteers. The session started with a great interest shown by the students, which boosted the volunteers. World class technologies and future modifications in the field of Robotic sciences were explained in that session. The head of the organization started collecting the feedbacks from the students regarding the session performed. He found a boy, sitting with a dull expression and seemed to be irritated. The organizing head went near the boy and asked,"What's the matter champ? Is everything ok? Did you feel the importance of the session?" and was shocked by the reply. "What's the use of learning these things which will never help me in the future. I don't even feel interested to engage with my studies"..

"I agree the words that you didn't like the session. What will you do in the future without a degree?", the head asked him.. "I want to become a politician, just like my father", he replied.......

ᐅᐅᐅ

This is a true incident, where the organizing head is my colleague. This incident protrayed the thoughts of the young people, whom we thought would be the backbone of the country. This story made me to analyze the importance of "Public administration, political science, History, Civics and Economics" in the growing world.

3

Liquidating Creativity

" We are educating people out of their creative capacities..........I believe this passionately, that we don't grow into creativity, we grow out of it. Or rather, we get educated out of it.
Ken Robinson.."

Many commercial educational institutions committed the crime of killing creativity of students. If killing the ideas of an individual is declared to be a crime, by the law, most of the people would be residing in the prison. The community(Society) itself is not ready to accept the idea of Creativity. All they prefer is to copy from an obtained sources because, it is the most easy suggestion that can be given. This is the only reason for the underrated development of our country, not in my view, but in every Indian's opinion.

36% of Indian scientists at NASA, who stood the example for their hard and creative work with the best outputs, never made India feel proud. Because, they were indulged in the activities of a foreign organization, which gave importance to their ideas. Mars rover, SpaceX-Demo 2 were some examples describing the great works of Indians, but the credit goes to their country. Companies and organisations equal to the capabilities of Google, Microsoft, Adobe and many would have emerged in India, but, it's we, who made it move away from our hands.

Settlement is given importance rather than success, thinking that getting succeeded is a time consuming process.We, the young people of India, got irritated by listening, **"Get settled in your life,**

prefer the job and get a better settlement, work here,work there, do this, do that and all you need is settlement".........because, settlement is what we enjoy our own but, success is what makes the community develop. Majority of the young people of our country are preferring to shape our country to the best they can. The recent surveys and research made it clear that youngsters are making their lives to live for the development of the nation. The emerging startups are the examples. Liquidating creativity of a person is just like murdering a person itself. But mankind gets extincted by the time we realize the truth.

An astronaut, whose dreams were all around the stars, was striving hard , in calculating the resistance values in his electrical machines laboratory. A future scientist, who wanted to invent medicine for cancer, was now a pharmacist, selling medicines. A girl, who thought herself as an upcoming doctor, to serve the nation, was fighting for her own life at the jaws of death, just because of the pressure of her parents, who forced her to become a CA. This is not what happenned in the past or else not predicting the future. It's all what is happenning every day, every hour, every minute, every second and each and every moment.

Present trend of

Indian Education

These training skills may provide the ability to solve the problems in subjects, but it fails to train the students, face the problems in their life. This failure and inability made India stand at the top in Suicide rate. Though India would be the nation with more number of youngsters in the future, they will be just robots, performing their assigned task and activities just like programmed machines. A nation should be capable of taking their own decisions but not performing the signified tasks. It just resembles the factory, where machines work to produce an output.

We want a Versatile society, moving with a rapid pace of Development, but not a factory, producing programmed objects, performing the operations commanded by its master.

Remember, we are an independent nation now. We don't need Technology to be implemented all over the country. Remember the days of our ancestors without dependence on technlogy. Human is capable of doing everything. Why we need a machine to help us at such instance?????????

❧❧❧

4
The Gender Criteria

Savitribai phule, the mother of Indian feminism and her husband Jyotirao phule, who took the lead of women's emancipation in India, are the real icons behind the thought of feminism. Girls, who are going to schools, colleges and woman, who are engaged in work, should thank these people for their sacrifice.

Women, during the vedic period, were accessed with best education patterns and gradually, they lost their right. This declined idea got it's revival by the social movements led by **Raja Ram**

Mohan Roy and Iswar chandra Vidyasagar. Woman in the field of Science and Technology, space sciences, Law, Social sciences and many.....are the examples for their great works. But, not each and every girl of India is accessed with education.**Gender discrimination**, the most peculiar concept is the only reason. Women were thought to be inferior, from ancient days to till now. No literary works of the past stated the reason behind the concept of gender supremacy but, it all happenned at a pace.

Many of the girls, who dreamt of being an engineer, a doctor, an astronaut, a scientist, an entrepreneur and many, were confined to the walls of their houses. Their dreams, left them unsuccessful in their lives, resulting in the underrated development of women empowerment. This condition got improved. Women got engaged in many milestones of Indian history. They took part in improving the national integrity. But, what happenned to our country in this recent times......???.....The saviors of the world are striving to live, live in an odd community where women are not given any importance and trying to make themselves survive in a society of vultures hunting on them.

"
यत्र नार्यसत् पूज्ययन्त रमनत तत्र दवेता:।
यत्रेतासत् न पूज्ययन्त सर्वासततराफला: क्रयिा:। "

"Where Women are honoured, divinity blossoms there, and where ever women are dishonoured, all action no matter how noble it may be, remains unfruitful".

-Manusmrithi

Women are still facing such situation, especially in remote and rural areas, where most of the population are illiterate. "Education" matters everything. If they would have known the importance of education, all the people over there would have accessed to it.

If we observe the news papers, posts on social media and other information sources, we can see the editorials describing the greatness of the particular woman assigned with an activity, in her field of interest. **"Why? Why such news is being highlighted? Aren't they capable of performing that work? Don't they suit to that work?"** It's all because of the feeling of gender supremacy. Nothing is impossible and difficult for a woman, who became a warrior by giving birth to the child.

Sex education should be made into a subject that helps the students to learn the basic principle of livelihood but, our so called educationalists raise their doubt regarding the advantages of implementing and promoting it as a subject. "Dear brothers of young India...Explain these illiterates who ask such silly questions that **"Education is to promote ourselves out of the chained borders of Illiteracy but not to make ourselves rich because, education is our right, not a commodity"**. Many private organisations and startups were involved in the activity to promote Sex education. Creating awareness regarding sex education should be our responsibility.....................

ᐅᐅᐅ

((I have seen many such activities of creating awareness regarding sex education and its importance, but the campaign lead by the students of ISB(**ICFAI Bussiness School)** created a great impact on my ideology........))

ᐅᐅᐅ

5

The closed room combat

Every boy, who enjoys the game play of our cricketers, would have dreamt of their presence in the middle of the stadium, holding the bad and his name being chanted among the crowd. Every girl, who had gone through the live telecast of P.V. Sindhu's felicitation ceremony for her Olympic medal, would have thought herself as a champion and to make India proud.......But, the sad endings of their dreams are that they are confined to their rooms, with a heap of books infront of them......I remember the words of my neighbour, on the day when Abhinav Bindhra won the olympic gold medal, **"India need this boosting....our government should support more players so that more medals can be won...."**, then, I asked him what does he want his son to do and he replied, **"An engineer"**..... We, the people of India, always strive for the best output, but never tries to supply the best and pure raw material.....

That's the only reason, millions of millennials were confined to the closed rooms, surviving their lives, just for their parents and to fulfill their dreams. Parents were thinking that their children were performing good in their academics, but deep inside, the students were fighting the greatest battles with their mind. No student is allowed to explore the outer world. **"Study, study, study......"** and no other allegations to be carried...... Then, how can we get a Rahul dravid for the future, if play ground was just a subject illustration shown in the book.

I termed this phenomena as "Pressure cooker survival", which is mostly found in............**"Indian educational sytem"**. "Privatization of educational institutions" is the major reason for the implementation of survival games, which made a great death toll all through the years.........

A letter to the survivor:

"

My Dear brothers and sisters,

I have heard about many freedom fighters, who sacrificed their lives for our better livelihood. But, the people of our country don't deserve it. Atleast, we would have been safe, if the British rule continued till now. Now, I see the real warriors, fighting for their own livelihood and freedom, in an independent country and that's you. But remember, it's just like questing for pure water in a sea. All your dreams meant to be packed in the bag. You should never attempt the crime, letting it out. Your dreams aren't valuable compared to the dreams of your parents, who wanted to make you an engineer or a doctor. Even if the god comes before them and ask them to have a wish, they want these wishes to be fulfilled. The moment you are born is the moment your designation is fixed. Before the naming ceremony, they decides the degree you should pursue in the future. The story books are replaced with the quantum physics text books, encyclopedia occupies the place of the drawing book, Online classes appears on the screen where you wanted to have the cartoon serials. Your life appears professional at a very young age. Your language proficiency increases, which make you an intellectual.

The moment you have everything I mentioned above, you will be having a question, deep inside your mind, " Did I become Professional, what my parents wanted?" and the cute little answer is "YES" but when it comes to you, you will realise about your lost childhood......

You lived the life of your parents all the 25 years, fighting for their dreams, questing the methods that satisfy them, living in the environment designed by your mentors. Simply saying, you are just an actor and just acted according to the designed script. You are just a puppette all through the life of yours. Time gets lapsed by the time you get realized. What will be the next????? You get married and give birth to children and the drama continues. You will frame the script, in which your child will be the actor of it. The trend continues..........resulting in the land of people *with their dreams assassinated. India will be called as " Land of dead dreams", if this trend continues.........*

What is the remedy of this problem?????? Fight for your dream comrades. Nothing is most precious than desire, nothing is important than your target and nothing is prominent infront of your ambition. It will be your first crime when you hesitate to express your Idea. Though you are alive physically, you are dead in your dream land.

Be the real warrior, which makes you the role model to the future generations. It may hurt the feelings of your parents, but, it will be a great loss in the future, if you remain silent. No parent will be the threat to their children. They just want to make the life of their children free from the challenges they faced in their future.

Run like a cheetah on synthetic turves and grasslands, jump like a tiger, concentrate like a lion, think like a fox, burn like a sun and make yourself connected to the way to fulfill your dreams.

#FIGHT_FOR_DREAMS

- The millennial Representative"

6

The overweighted responsibility

Looking at 20 books in the bag of a 1st class kid, reminds me, a worker carrying a cotton sack. Thank god, Atleast, the school uniform differentiated them. Students turned into professional labourer. It was still funny when my friend wished me "Happy Labour day", when we were pursuing our 10th class. The time moved on and bags became sacks..

Rendezvous with Haversack

((It's an interview cabin of a news channel. With lights around, the anchor of the news channel, occupied his seat. Cameras rolled and the live telecast started))

Anchor: Good morning everyone. This is your Reporter Vishwa and you are watching **"The Millennial News"**. Today, we are going to interview an icon of todays world, **"The Bag"**......... Lets welcome him with a big round of applause.

((The entry of our subject from the applause at the back side))

The bag: Good morning one and all. Thanks for your love and your affection, that made me occupy the best position in my life.

Anchor: (With an astonishing tone) May be, you are not aware of the causes that made your presence here, Mr. Bag...... You will get everything known by the end of the interview.....

The bag: (In Dilemma) The causes.....???? Ok, whatever it may be...... I am thankful for calling me for this interview.....

Anchor: Ok Mr. Bag, tell me what made you so prominent in everyone's live?

The bag: To explain this answer, I need to go to my past. Gunny bag, my ancestor, once conducted a council meeting with the remaining bags in his community. He felt very bad as they were just confined to carry vegetables, commodities and goods. He tried very hard for the improvement of our lives. He motivated the future generations and it's what we are now at present.

Anchor: I have never heard such a motivating story in my life..... You are so much thankful to your ancestors. Isn't it?

The bag: (with a smile) Not only our community of school bags, but also the community of Plasic bags, carrier bags, sacks and many, are thankful to our ancestors. Because of them, we had our own identity.

Anchor: Let's get into your personal life. How is your life, Mr. Bag?

The bag: My life is very pleasant and good. I have a very good body design and assigned to an unique activity of carrying books. It's a privilege to be to bear the weights of the healthy living of Future generations.

Anchor: That's good, Mr. Bag. So, you think, you are the reason for the healthy future. But, do you know the real fact, that's deep inside a student's mind?

The bag: What a silly question......(with a continuous smile) Why wouldn't I know the things in their mind? We often talk with our companion. The only thing they say at the last is "You are heavy and I can't bear you".

Anchor: What will you do then? Don't you feel pity of their conditions they are suffering. Don't you think that you are the reason for their suffering?

The bag: Yeah, I feel pity of those shoulders, which carry me without a hesitation. I feel pity of the back bone, which gave me a support to get fixed, without any disturbance. I feel pity of those tiny legs, bearing the heavy weights and those cute little eyes, filled with tears of pain.

I feel angry upon myself, for being a great burden to the young people, at a very young age. Not only me, but everyone of our community feels the same pain, for letting our heavy weights creating burden to those young minds. But, we have nothing to do. It's all because, we are assigned with the activity of carrying books, but we are not mentioned with the particular weights that are to be carried. .It's our fundamental duty. Our ethics are no more useful. We want to wipe their tears, but don't have hands. We want to comfort them with our words, but we gave no mouth to speak.

At first, we thought, though we were heavy, we were just contributing a best future. Later, when we had a look at the books we were carrying, we felt the real pain. Those books are of no use. We realized that we carried the study materials, which helped them as instant preparation materials. We would have felt happy if we carried the text books.

It's all because of the school managements, we had a disgrace in the society. Not even thinking and analyzing the prominence of the particular book, the management takes the decision of placing us in the bag. Just tell me what's the use of "An Encyclopedia" or else a "Dictionary" in the bag of an elementary student.

Government took many decisions of reducing our weights and we are even carrying our diet restrictions. We found no response from the management of various institutions. An idea created a great impact that "Carrying large sum of books results in a good future".......
But, they never observed the health impacts that rises in the future. To your kind information, we feel the real pain. The bags feel the real pain. But, we never had the chance to express it. It's because of you people, I represented the feeling of each and every bag in our community.

Anchor: We thought you, as the threat to children and school students but, your words make me realise the mistake. We got known that the privatization of educational institutions is the reason for the problem, that is being faced by the students. Thank you a lot, Mr. Bag, for being the representative of your community and for the great words.

The bag: Thank you very much, Vishwa, for creating a platform to express my ideas. Thank you, **"The Millennial News"** for the opportunity.....

(The live session ends with the claps of the crew, with a teary eyes)

ᐯᐯᐯ

What's in your mind, Readers? Whom do you feel the threat to healthy education? Do you accept the feelings of the Bag? .... Just quest for the answers to the questions that are rolling in your mind.....

ᐯᐯᐯ

7

The Social "Media" Distancing

Mobile phones created a great impact on everyone's life by connecting us, to the world. It became a reliable source of information and tera bytes of Data. It lead to the electronic revolution, changing the configurations of the world. Simply saying, "world in an electronic box" is what phone called. Creating a good relation with the corners of the world, phones aparted us from our own people, that's what I call **SMD (Social Media Distancing)".** We don't have the ability to create a new social platform, but stands at the first in using. A connecting device became conqueror of the world. **"How shame it is for us to be ruled by a lifeless creature...."**but, no one cares.

Shopping, playing, studying, searching and whatelse remained?... Everything got possibled by a mobile phone. Creating such device is not a mistake. The usage of it makes such fault. It's not our fundamental duty to use mobile phones on roads, not our right, to use it day and night continuously and not at all written in our Constitution, that phones are compulsory for every student. It has become a major leap and prominent source in the evolution of life.

Spending time got easier with a phone, making the book, meant for the book rack. PDF's are ruling the world of book reading. Electronic mails were laughing at the post letters and made telegrams to commit suicide. Virtual playgrounds are attracting the children, who left aside the normal playgrounds, making it invaded by the weed.

A day in the future......(Lives of the virtual world)

Toddlers got more attracted to mobile phones. Parents found it easier to manage their children by making them attracted to the virtual world. Even during the time of eating, they prefer watching video clips and cartoon shows. It's not about one, but, I am talking about everyone. Though phones are meant to communicate, it got upgraded. Simply saying, it became a companion in our life. **"People started loving mobile phones and ignored people"**.........

Millennials prefer to share their feelings, thoughts and ideas on the social platform, but what made them to ignore their fellow people...... The most common answer we hear at that moment is " Sry, I am busy"......... and again start's typing on their phone. Even a minute appears very hard, leaving their phones.

Let's have a look at the busy schedule of our young people......

- Googling the phone for unimportant stuff and useless things
- watching shows on OTT platforms
- Chit-chatting with friends and collegues
- Playing games

.... so on.........

Does any activity among the listed things, is important, that make a person busy.....????? You don't even find a single thing, because, all these are just the reasons of execuses, just to escape from the real world.

"My dear future of the nation. People in our lives are meant to share our feelings. They are just like a boat to make us reach the other end of the river bank. Half of the day is spent by looking at the phone itself. Remember about your family. Why can't you be active in helping your mother in household works, your father in gardening and your siblings in playing???..... You find it pleasant, being active in the online platform, but remember, being active in real time is the best thing that is appreciable......."......

We usually see people, especially college students, rejecting the phone calls of their parents, siblings and friends while they are busy playing. I think, most of the people have experienced this situation and most of them stood the reason of someone's experience...... Remember, you are not ignoring a call, you are ignoring the life of a person.

ᑭᑭᑭ

Let's talk about a situation faced by a girl. Shresta, a girl from Delhi, who was passionate in Astronomy and space, went to a science seminar that was conducted at science centre, which was far from her house. She never thought about the delay and the seminar got terminated at 9:45 PM. Everyone started their way to home. Shresta called her parents to inform them about the delay, so that her parents never get worried. The phone was picked up by her brother Anshu as her parents left the phone in the house and went to a marriage ceremony. She informed him about the delay in the seminar and informed him that she started her journey on her scooty. On the middle of the way, she was hitted by a car and got hurt very badly. The road was silent and the car ran away without even slowing down. Shresta tried hard to get her phone from the bag and called her brother. His brother, who was busy playing "PUBG", ignored her call thinking that she would tell a reason for her late arrival again. Shresta tried again and again but her brother didn't lift the call. Shresta became unconscious and fainted. Some people, who were going on that way, found her lying on the road, admitted her in the hospital. Thank god, Shresta is safe but her brother can't forget the mistake he did. He would have lost his sister, due to his negligence.

ÞÞÞ

A boy named Arjun, was in a bad mood on that day, as he got failed to get selected in his college science fair. He worked very hard to make it successful but it didn't meet the standards of the panel of judges. Though he was comforted by his friends and fellow classmates, he was unable to recover from it. He cried all the day. He called his friend Harshit, but he didn't get connected with him. Later, he received a message from Harshit that he was busy in a chit chat with his female friend and also said that he would call later. Arjun called his sister Varsha, but she rejected his call as she was busy watching a web series. Arjun got depressed at that moment but he didn't make a call to his parents as he don't wanted to trouble them. He found no solution to get out of it and decided to commit suicide. Arjun was no more.

Stories are pleasant to hear but no of this kind. Take a moment, just a moment to talk to your well wishers. Your words may be the medicine to cure the pain inside. You can share your feelings, emotions and best moments on social media but not with the mobile phone. Just leave it aside, thinking it as a medium of conversation. Stay a bit close to your favourite people...and it will be the best medicine, for both......

ÞÞÞ

8
Students or Printing machines?

I don't know, whether the educational institutions of India got inspired by Sir Johannes Gutenberg, promoting the manufacture of printing machines. Children are turned into printing machine by the newly formulated technical concepts and education patterns. The teachers, who are meant to teach the subject, started delivering the thing directly, looking at the textbook. Not even uttering a single mistake while delivering, them are thinking themselves as intellectuals. Text book is a source for the teacher, to give an explaination and it's a learning guide for the students. But, everything got transformed to the most worst situation.

My friend faced such situation during his college study. He had a professor for "Signals and systems", who always delivered his lecture looking at his text book. I won,t say it an act of Delivering but it's an act of reading. He never explained a single concept regarding the subject but went on reading the paragraphs. He also wanted his lecture to be noted in the note book. My friend, who was fed up with his lecturer's teaching pattern, stopped writing the notes of his lecture and sat silently. His professor observed him for some time without uttering a word. After sometime he made him stand and asked him the reason for his negligence regarding noting the lecture. My friend replied, **"I don't find it useful, sir. I was just writing every line of the text book that you are delivering. I can even do the same thing looking at the text book in the library. We are staying in the class rooms so that we could know something in detail regarding the subject. But what we are doing is just producing 60 more textbooks"**. His lecturer got angry upon him and complained the Dean about his argument. Thank god, the dean was educated. He found the fault in the teaching pattern of the professor and warned him to change his way of teaching.........

There is another thing which relates to our subject, that is to be considered ....**"The Laboratory Records"**.........Half of the college life of the students get submerged in writing the laboratory observations and records. Laboratories are meant to experience the real life experiences and case study but due to this fear of writing the useless scripts, most of the college students prefer to skip their laboratory periods as they find it useless...... **"If lab records are removed from the college acdemics, the students will find more leisure time and they can carry the works of their interests. Rather than writing a record, it is very easy to write a 3 to 4 fictional books in a semester"** said my friend.

These experiences reflects the real fault in our education system. Copying a book from the source and copying a case study from wikipedia sources is not at all fair for the students, who mean the backbone of our country. I heard the words of some mentors that **"Even our constitution was copied from the constitutions of different countries. So, what is the mistake of suggesting students to write their assignments, records and case studies from the sources?"** ...." **To all the illiterates and fools of our society, Constitution was copied to have the best patterns of ruling. It was derieved from the best. If we talk about the records, we are just talking about the useless scrap. Constitution is framed for our better livelihood and how useful are the records and observations in our real life????? Just use brains to design a better livelihood and in designing a beautiful future.**

ᐅᐅᐅ

9

English...English...English....

Language, the medium to exchange our felings and emotions. Language, the most powerful weapon of an intellectual. Language, the most preferred parameter to estimate the performance of a person. Language, the representative of a state and a country. Language became most prominent in our day to day life. Language helped many, to design their lives. Language changed many things, even our love towards our mother tongue. It all started at the schools, promoting English learning methodologies. It became a sign of pride to the parents, whose children were trained to speak in English, rather than their mother tongue. It's even digrace to hear children calling their parents "Mom and Dad" besides the words "Amma and Nanna". Speaking in English may give us respect in other countries, but we should remember the thing that we are causing disrespect to our mother tongue.

At present, English became more prominent in every aspect of our livelihood. Many companies are looking for students, who are fluent in using English language. If someone asks for the reason behind the failure in campus drive, the answer we obtain is "Lack of English fluency"..... It's not due to lack of English fluency but lack of Communication skills. English is not at all a language or a dialect, that belong to India. It's a communication medium we inherited from the British rule. It doesn't mean to put our mother tongue out of our reach. Remember the moment you get hurted by something, you will realise how our lives interlinked with our mother tongue.

Friends, acquaintance, collegues, relatives and even children started exchanging their ideas in English. Those words just appear as words but dont deliver the feeling, that's deep inside our mind. Though we try hard to get the best knowledge in English, we failed to acquire it. It's due to inefficiency of schooling and incapability of our teacher community. It's very funny to see a person of my age teaching students in the private schools. How can he acquire the calibre, that makes him to teach students effectively. The college students, who came from English medium, are trying hard to communicate with the foreign ambassadors during the workshop sessions. This shows our incapability.......

Who are we to think English is the langugae that makes us look official?? Remember the day 11 September 1893, where Swami Vivekananda addressed the people of Chicago with his warm greeting **"Sisters and brothers of America"**..... It's not about the language used but it's all about the formal way he acquired to address the fellow men and women. It all rises deep from the heart. Remember that it can't be made possible by foreign languages. I request the teachers not to strive hard, speaking the butler English and guide the student to learn the most sacred mother tongue...

""For us Indians, I don't think English can ever exude that magic of emotions which our mother tongue can."

- Kailash Kher"

Afterword

To the readers,

Everyone has their own experiences regarding their schooling and college education. You may have suffered a lot by these education patterns but you can't do anything rather than remebering those dark days. Making those things highlighted, we can make a move towards stress free education. It's a great pain to see students committing suicide, just to escape from this pressure. Getting through many such real life experiences, I made my mind to deliver an anecdote which helps others to realise their mistakes.... Especially, I would like to address every parent of India. All the short stories inscribed in the book are true and nothing is imaginary, but the characters are replced by another name. Education became accessible to rich whereas Government institutions are failing to promote the right to education. Being a responsible citizen of India, I wanted this book to change the ideology of each and every individual and make everyone to follow their dreams. Literary works like Books help to create a greater awareness than that of Social media and blogs. This is the only reason that made me to write a book.

Conclusion

India, as described earlier, should be the sign of "Enriched Education" with Ethics and Human values. This is not for an individual, but it helps in framing a good community with a rich heritage. Sir A.P.J. Abdul kalam dreamt of well developed nation by 2020, where he believed that the young people of India would be the supporters. But, our youngsters are busy using their phones to explore the virtual world rather than preferring to live in real world. This book may or may not help the young people to realise their mistake, but it's our responsibility to create awareness through all possible challenges.

All this is to achieve **#Vision_2020.** Dream lies within everyone and it's also we, who should strive to fulfill it. If no one cares, it's not a mistake of our's. It's the mistake of their ideology and their incapability to fulfill their dreams. Depending on others appear easier, but being a leader is the toughest thing. It's the chioce of every individual of being a host or a parasite. Aim for high taht makes you unique.......

To all the young soldiers, who are reading this book. Be the best version of you to frame a healthy environment, which itself helps to create a healthy nation........

#Vision_2020
#Education_for_all